Captured Moment

Snowflakes dance l
Frosty noses turning red as clowns.
People slip and tumble on the ground,
While snowmen chuckle, joy abound.

Sleds zoom by, a wild race unfolds,
Hot cocoa spills, but who cares, we're bold.
Bunnies leap, their fur all askew,
Ignoring the chill, we make quite a view.

Icicles hang like frozen guitars,
As snowball fights wage, we’re all rockstars.
The laughter echoes, light and clear,
Winter's a hoot, let's all give a cheer!

So raise your cup, let’s toast the snow,
To frosty adventures, we’ll let laughter flow.
Captured moments, each giggle sublime,
In this frozen wonder, we’ll dance through time.

The Breath of Subzero Dreams

Penguins waddle with a haughty sway,
Curtains of frost, they steal the play.
Dreams of sun, but here we are,
Sipping chill drinks beneath a star.

Frostbitten fingers hold a cup too tight,
As snowflakes tumble, what a sight!
Chattering teeth join the festive song,
In this winter wonder, we all belong.

Polar bears lounge on their frozen beds,
Imagining picnics with cozy spreads.
While frosty breath becomes a cloud,
Winter's parade, oh so proud.

Let’s build a fire, roast marshmallows fat,
Witty jokes fly, how about that?
It’s chilly out, but that’s just fine,
We’ll snuggle together, sip warm wine.

Solstice Stillness

Stillness blankets the frosty ground,
While squirrels chatter, lost and found.
Winter's antics, a comic play,
As icicles dangle, glistening gray.

Jackets puffed like marshmallow fluff,
Tripping on ice, it's never enough!
Every step feels like a big show,
With hilarious slips that steal the glow.

The sun peeks shy behind clouds of gray,
Tickling the earth with warmth's ballet.
But sweaters reign in this chilly spree,
We're all just penguins, can't you see?

Giggles bubble amidst the snow,
As we embrace the frosty flow.
In this season of shrieks and delight,
We'll belly-laugh 'til the stars are bright.

Fragments of Frostbitten Memories

Memory flakes fall like glitter bright,
As kids parade in a snowball fight.
Sleds crash, laughter fills the air,
While mom’s hot soup is beyond compare.

Snowmen grinning with button eyes,
As we try to build the ultimate prize.
But half the carrot ends up in a bite,
Oh, the joys of this chilly night!

Wrapped up tight, with hats askew,
The adventure brings laughter, ever new.
Snapshots of winter, so much to share,
Each shivering hug shows we care.

So let’s make more, both silly and sweet,
In this wintry realm, let’s not miss a beat.
We'll gather these moments, our hearts entwined,
In this frosted fun, joy we'll find.

Icicles and Intrigues

Icicles hang, all pointy and mean,
The sneaky squirrels plan a heist unseen.
With every drip, they whisper a plot,
To steal a snack—oh, who'd have thought!

Snowmen gather, plotting their reign,
While kids throw snowballs, causing some pain.
The carrot noses twitch with a scheme,
As they conspire in a frosty dream.

Penguins shuffle, waddle, and dance,
In a chilly contest—give them a chance!
With their tuxedo suits, oh what a sight,
They aim for the ice crown, all through the night!

Thus, winter rumbles, full of delight,
With characters plotting from morning till night.
Enjoy the chaos that it brings,
In this snowy land, oh how the laughter sings!

Embrace of the Winter Night

The moonlight casts a silver sheen,
While snowflakes twirl, a ballerina scene.
A yeti grins from the mountain high,
As snowmen giggle, waving goodbye.

Hot cocoa waits in mugs so bold,
With marshmallow smiles against the cold.
But a squirrel leaps with a daring flair,
To steal those treats—oh, the audacity rare!

Kids bundled up, an army of fun,
Building forts and snowballs until they're done.
A snowball fight breaks out in a flash,
Laughter echoes with every splash!

So dance through the flurries, let good times blend,
With winter antics that never seem to end.
In this playful chill, hearts can ignite,
Creating memories under stars so bright!

Nebula of Snowflakes

Each snowflake falls, a unique little gem,
As children catch them with a joyful hem.
They wonder aloud, 'What shape will they be?'
A glittering storm, oh so silly and free!

The snow drifts pile with a crinkle and crunch,
As dogs dash through, they tumble and munch.
With their floppy ears flapping like kites,
They plunge into snowdrifts in playful delights!

A fashion show struts, all bundled and tight,
With hats too big, what a comical sight!
They twirl in their boots, with scarves that unfurl,
In this wintry wonder, let laughter swirl!

They dance on the ice, twirling with glee,
While parents just watch, rolling their eyes, oh me!
Yet hearts are warm as the cold winds blow,
In the nebula bright, where memories grow!

The Stillness Before the Thaw

The world is hushed, a blanket of white,
Snowflakes settle in whispers of night.
An owl hoots softly, a wise old sage,
While rabbits ponder and turn a new page.

A bear snores loud, tucked tight in his den,
Dreaming of berries and sunshine again.
But winter giggles, no hurry to part,
As frost paints cheeky designs on each heart.

A pair of ice skates just long for the glide,
While children are scheming for slippery rides.
They gather their courage, take off without fear,
And tumble like chubby little deer!

Thus, chaos awaits as the temperatures rise,
Nature stirs softly, opens its eyes.
Embrace the stillness, for thrills lie in store,
With laughter and fun, winter never is a bore!

Frosted Dreams and Fading Light

Snowflakes dance on heads so bare,
Frosty breath fills the chilly air.
Hot cocoa spills, a chocolate mess,
Laughter erupts, who would have guessed?

Sledding down hills, a slippery race,
We tumble and roll, lose all our grace.
A snowman blinks, but it’s just our friend,
Who would’ve thought the snow would descend?

Icicles hang like frozen spears,
Pointing out dangers, fueling our fears.
But we still try to take that brave leap,
And laugh as we slide down, a tummy-deep heap!

In fluffy layers, we waddle around,
Tripping and giggling, plopping on ground.
The frosty air sings, loud and bright,
Let’s embrace this chill with all our might!

Serenity in Silver

The world is wrapped in a frosty hug,
Snowflakes swirl like a cozy rug.
But snowmen frown, as they slowly melt,
Their carrot noses, an icy belt!

We build a fort, like kings in dreams,
But a snowball fight's bursting at the seams.
Squeals of delight echo in the cold,
As laughter makes memories we'll hold.

A snow shovel sits, all covered in fluff,
And David builds high, shouting, "That's enough!"
When plow trucks roll, we feel the gloom,
But who can resist a snow-day's bloom?

In the silver glow of our playful plays,
We find joy in the chill, those winter days.
With hearts so bright, we embrace the freeze,
For happiness flows like a gentle breeze!

The Winter's Lament

Oh winter, you come with your frosty charms,
But do you have to freeze all our arms?
Hot chocolate spills, oh what a mess,
Next time, I swear I won't wear this dress!

The squirrels have hidden all their nuts,
While we're stuck grumbling in icy ruts.
We sip on soup and try to stay warm,
Watching snowflakes perform their storm!

Snow boots squeak like a funny tune,
While ice skaters slip, but who needs a boon?
Shovels in hand, as we trudge along,
Trying to find where we all belong!

With scowls and grins, we battle the chill,
Dreams of summer give us a thrill.
Oh winter, dear friend, why must you tease?
For laughter and joy, we'll always appease!

Twilight of the Frozen Woods

As daylight fades, the world turns white,
Creatures darting, a whimsical sight.
Under the stars, a snowball flies,
And laughter ignites, echoing the skies.

The owls hoot with a quirky flair,
While penguins waddle without a care.
Frosty branches wear coats of glass,
And winter pixies shine as they pass!

Chasing our dreams through fields of snow,
We trip on our faces, and up we go!
With mittens lost and noses so red,
We gather round fires, where stories are spread.

Twilight descends, oh what a treat,
As we dance with the chill that tickles our feet.
With cheers and giggles, we bow to the night,
For winter's grimace is a comic delight!

A Web of White Over the World

Snowflakes dancing like they're in a show,
Covering rooftops, making them glow.
Sleds zooming by with giggles and glee,
Hot cocoa spills, oh, what a sight to see!

Snowmen with noses made out of coal,
Wobbly hats that can’t take the toll.
Snowball fights where no one can score,
Laughter resounds, who could ask for more?

Icicles glisten, but they’re quite a tease,
One sharp drop, and you’re done with the freeze.
Winter jackets like marshmallows pound,
Can’t find my feet, where’s solid ground?

Yet in this chill, we dance with delight,
Embracing the frost, oh what a night!
With cheeks rosy red, we jump and we play,
Who needs the sun on a snowy day?

Through the Window of Stillness

Through glass panes fogged with a warming breath,
I see the kids plotting, avoiding the depth.
In tiny boots, they crunch and they trudge,
Making snow angels, just a quiet grudge.

Cats huddle tight, in blankets they'll hide,
While dogs chase their tails, full of goofy pride.
Puddles freeze under a curtain of white,
Watch your step now, it’s a slippery sight!

The squirrel on the branch slips with great flair,
He gives a glare that asserts his despair.
Snowflakes are falling, but oh what a fuss,
Nature’s confetti, no need to discuss!

But here in the warmth, with cocoa and cheer,
We sip and we laugh, and forget all the fear.
Cheers to the chill that makes memories bright,
Now tell me, who doesn’t love snowy delight?

Glassy Paths beneath Winter's Spell

Sidewalks like mirrors, reflecting the trees,
One wrong step and you're down on your knees!
Skates on the pond, spinning like tops,
Laughter erupts as someone just plops!

Hot tea and mittens, my hands can't get warm,
But outside they're sliding in a snowy swarm.
Penguin-waddles and snowflakes that fall,
"Catch me if you can!"—oh, that's the call.

Down little hills, they dash and they gleam,
Oh what a riot, this whole winter dream!
Joyous shouts echo through frosty air,
Winter brings laughter, who could despair?

Yet inside I ponder, the chips on my plate,
Will I indulge? Or shall I just wait?
In this frosted kingdom, each giggle a treat,
We feast on hot snacks while embracing the heat.

The Art of Winter's Solitude

Snow blankets silence, a hush like a tune,
Sipping my coffee, while birds hum a swoon.
The world seems to pause, not a soul in sight,
Just me and my thoughts in the fading light.

But wait, here appears a ruckus outside,
Ah, those energetic kids take the slide!
Wheels and sleds stacked, a winter parade,
Laughter explodes, my quiet charade.

Snowflakes huge, as if they’re in a race,
Grumbling about how they’ve lost their place.
Fluttering down, they make a grand dance,
And I find myself pulled, caught in the chance.

So here’s to the cold, and the fun it brings,
In frosty embraces, even solitude sings.
Life’s silly moments tucked under the stars,
Are better with laughter, no matter how far!

Beneath the Blanket of White

Snowflakes dance like they've lost their minds,
Sleds on rooftops, oh what fun it finds!
The snowman grins with a carrot nose,
Wondering where the sunshine goes.

Hot cocoa spills on a woolly sock,
Penguins in parades, who needs a dock?
I'm wearing boots that are two sizes too big,
Slip, slide, and laugh, oh what a gig!

Footprints lead to places unknown,
A snowball fight, and my cover's blown!
Chasing my friends in a flurry of white,
Winter's just silly, what a delight!

Oh, tuck me in, I'm cozy and bright,
Wrapped in layers, a marshmallow sight.
With laughter like snowflakes that tumble and sway,
Let's make winter a game, hooray!

When Spring Waits Indefinitely

The calendar's stuck, oh what a scene,
Spring’s playing hide and seek, unseen.
My garden’s still frozen, a popsicle patch,
I’m convinced it's a prank, a seasonal catch!

Is that a bud, or a snowdrift’s tease?
I sip on soup while the trees sneeze.
Where did the tulips go, what a plight,
I swear they’ve run off, oh what a fright!

The sun plays peekaboo, with a cloud's sly grin,
And I’m in a parka, where’s the warmth you’ve been?
I bought new flip-flops, just last week,
Yet here I am, in socks that squeak!

I’ll twirl with the squirrels in a woolly hat,
Turning my frown into friendship with that!
If spring’s waiting forever, let’s throw a bash,
In snow boots and shorts, let’s make a splash!

The Dance of the Winter Moon

The moon’s throwing a party, oh what a sight,
Dressed in shiny frost, glowing so bright.
It winks at the pine trees, all dressed in frost,
“Let’s dance!” it whispers, “What a line lost!”

Snowflakes twirl, in a frosty ballet,
While I trip on my boots, oh that’s how I play!
Icicles drum on the roof like a band,
I grab my mittens, they’re close at hand!

A snowman’s a partner, with coal for a smile,
He spins me around — it’s a wobbly style.
Twilight giggles, the night’s full of cheer,
A symphony of winter sings loud and clear!

When the moon takes a bow and the stars align,
We’ll wrap up the dance in a woolly vine.
With giggles and snowflakes as our sweet boon,
Let’s give winter a shout-out, the dance of the moon!

Muffled Echoes in the Frost

Whispers of snow, oh listen so close,
The soft crunching sounds as it lightly dosed.
A dog’s snowy face, full of mischief and glee,
His paws are all soggy, did I mention that spree?

Hot soup’s for dinner, it warms me right through,
I can’t find my slippers, I think they blew!
The echoes of laughter bounce off frozen air,
As we pile up the snow in a laughter-filled lair!

The mailman now walks like he’s on a tightrope,
While I watch from my window, and can only hope.
That springtime arrives with a wink and a grin,
But winter's just funny, let the giggles begin!

So here’s to the frost that makes us all smile,
With memories of warmth stretching over a mile.
Laughter caught in cold, what a perfect blend,
Through muffled echoes, winter's our friend!

A Hearth's Warm Embrace

A hound curled tight by the fire's light,
With dreams of chasing squirrels all night.
The cat plots schemes with a sly little grin,
While visions of tuna dance in her chin.

The cocoa's swirling, marshmallows afloat,
Sipping too much, oh, what a to-do note!
The mugs keep clanking, laughter fills the room,
While dad's socks still rumble, his fashion's a gloom.

Outside the snow makes a soft, fluffy bed,
But the snowman has more style, or so I've said!
A carrot for a nose, and arms made of twigs,
Though he wears dad’s old hat, oh, how it digs!

Round the corner, a neighbor slips with a splash,
His dignity gone in a frosty flash!
We giggle and cheer from our windowed perch,
As he vows to conquer, and back he’ll lurch!

Frosted Pines and Moonlit Nights

The trees wear coats of powdery white,
While squirrels debate who's best in a fight.
Elves in the garden, they plot and they scheme,
To sneak in our snacks, what a holiday dream!

The moon's stealing glances, a playful old chap,
While snowflakes are dancing like kids on a lap.
Snowballs are thrown with great force and flair,
But the dog brings a snowball right back with a stare!

As night creeps in, the stars twinkle bright,
We build up a snow fort for playful delight.
The neighbors join in with their raucous cheer,
But they'll surely regret it come springtime, I fear!

With laughter and joy, the night doesn't end,
As we gather for cocoa, our favorite blend.
The chill is forgotten, the toast is in line,
As we toast to the frosty, the cozy, divine!

Lullabies of the Icy Breeze

The cold whispers secrets as it teases the night,
While penguins in PJs get ready for flight.
They huddle in circles, with straws for their drinks,
Sharing frosty stories that make all of us wink.

The wind plays a game with the chimes on the wall,
While laughter erupts from the far hallway's call.
Grandma's stories weave magic of old,
While hot apple cider warms hearts with its gold.

Outside, the frost bites, as kids leap about,
Giving frosty kisses, but never a pout.
They build up their castles, each tower a feat,
While claiming the yard as their own winter street.

In the twilight glow, with cheeks rosy and bright,
We cuddle up close, such a magical sight.
As stars wink above, like jokes shared between friends,
We drift off to dreams where the laughter never ends.

Dreaming Beneath a Crystal Sky

Under a canopy of twinkling stars,
We whisper our wishes and compare our cars.
The sleigh bells are jingling, but not from our ride,
It's Aunt Millie's knitting that's far from a guide!

With each frosty flake, we create such delight,
Like snowball catapults that soar into the night.
The neighbors are howling as snow lands with a thud,
While their dog looks bemused, half buried in mud.

The air's filled with giggles and festive good cheer,
While evenings grow longer, with snacks ever near.
Our mittens are soaking from snowball duels fought,
Yet laughter rings out, just like we always sought.

So curled up together, with warmth in our hearts,
We share silly tales and some berry tart parts.
For beneath this sky of crystal and light,
We're heroes of winter, with laughter in sight!

Glimmers of Hibernating Life

Beneath a blanket, snug and tight,
A bear dreams of candy every night.
Squirrels misplacing their own hidden stash,
While mice throw parties, making quite a splash.

The snowman wears the carrot with style,
Winking at the kids, it makes them smile.
With frosty breath they play and shout,
Hiding from snowballs flying about.

In every nook, some laughter brews,
A penguin slide on icy shoes.
Chasing snowflakes, a joyful race,
Winter's not sad, it’s a playful space.

So let’s embrace the frosty cheer,
With mittens on, let’s gather near.
For every shiver brings a fun surprise,
Warmth comes from laughter, laughter never lies.

The Lantern's Flicker in the Storm

A lantern flickers, casting light,
While down the street runs a frosty sprite.
He slips on ice, does a triple spin,
And lands in snow with a goofy grin.

A cat in boots sits by the door,
With paws like snow, she’s never a bore.
She plans a heist for the pie on the sill,
Her whiskers twitch as she waits for the thrill.

The winds howl fiercely, a raucous game,
As snowflakes join in, all dance the same.
Together they swirl, a merry parade,
With giggles and squeaks, no plans are delayed.

Beneath the storm's wild, frosty reach,
Silly tales become our speech.
With every gust, a chance to cheer,
Winter’s a stage that brings us near.

A Tapestry of Crystal Delights

Oh look at the trees, all sparkling bright,
They tip their branches, what a strange sight.
A choir of snowflakes, they sing with glee,
While rabbits are twirling like they’ve a degree.

Icicles hang like chandeliers grand,
As penguins waddle, making their stand.
A dance-off begins on the frozen pond,
With every misstep, a friendship is spawned.

Hot cocoa's brewing, let’s toast with cheer,
To marshmallows floating, they disappear!
Each cup is a canvas, painted with smiles,
In this wintry world, let's stay for a while.

So gather the laughter, the fun and the frost,
In this tapestry woven, we'll never be lost.
With a sprinkle of joy through the wintery night,
Let’s wrap ourselves in these pure delights.

Whispers of Winter's Exhale

Listen closely, can you hear that sound?
It’s winter giggling as it spins around.
The frost on windows, a funny tease,
While the dog chases snowflakes, with such ease.

Under the eaves, the ice drips away,
Melting in sunbeams, for some warmth today.
A raccoon sneaks out, eyes wild with mirth,
Claiming the yard is his own little Earth.

Snowman’s hat, now askew on his head,
He’s caught off guard, not ready for bed.
With a carrot nose that’s starting to droop,
He chuckles and sighs, joins the fun loop.

Though chilly winds may swish and sway,
There’s laughter hidden in the fray.
So let’s wrap up warm and laugh a while,
Finding joy in winter, that’s the true style.

Milton Keynes UK
Ingram Content Group UK Ltd.
UKHW022007131124
451149UK00013B/1048

Original title:
Moonlight on Ice

Author: Victor Mercer
ISBN HARDBACK: 978-9916-94-536-0
ISBN PAPERBACK: 978-9916-94-537-7

Frosted Dreams

Slippers slip on frozen ground,
I skate like a joyful clown.
Snowflakes fall, they dance and play,
I twirl and spin, then slide away.

My hat flies off, a silly sight,
Chasing it under stars so bright.
Hot cocoa spills, oh what a mess,
But laughter fills the coldness, yes!

Night's Gentle Hand

A squirrel skates with acrobatic flair,
His tiny tail dances in the air.
Penguin pals parade on the glint,
In their tuxedos, not a hint!

The owls hoot, they laugh aloud,
As frosty friends gather proud.
Bouncing off ice, the fun won't freeze,
As snowmen perform with perfect ease.

Serene Frostfire

A penguin takes a daring leap,
Into the ice, he makes a sweep.
His belly slides with a giggling sound,
While a bear stumbles, falls all around.

Frosty breath is seen in the air,
Chasing snowflakes without a care.
Laughter echoes through the night,
As winter antics spark delight.

Melodies of the Winter Moon

Hockey sticks made from marshmallow,
Shooting pucks shaped like a yellow.
The crowd of critters cheers in glee,
A game played under a dancing spree.

Twinkling lights laugh on every branch,
While joyful jubilance creates a ranch.
With each slide, a new joke told,
In this winter wonderland of old.

Secrets of the Starlit Sheet

Beneath the glow of silvery beams,
A penguin dances, or so it seems.
He slips and slides, what a sight!
I can't stop laughing, oh what a night!

His friends all cheer, they join the fun,
As frosty stars twinkle, one by one.
They all join in, a slippery race,
On this glistening runway, it’s a social space!

Whispered Chimes of the Cold

A chilly breeze whispers with glee,
As we try to skate, oh dear me!
Our noses red, our laughter bright,
Falling like snowballs in the night.

“Watch out!” I shout, as I glide by,
A tumble, a giggle, oh my, oh my!
Ice cream cones or ice-cold feet?
We'd choose the cones—now that's sweet!

Glittering Nightfall

On the sparkling path of tranquil white,
We wobble and tumble, what a sight!
One skater swirls like a fancy dress,
While eating snowflakes? Yes, I confess!

A snowball fight breaks out, oh no!
With giggles and shouts, we steal the show.
But hidden among chuckles, a slip and a roll,
Now that's the best punchline of the whole!

Frosted Echoes

Echoes of laughter bounce in the air,
As my buddy awkwardly lifts in despair.
Trying to skate, he’s a sight to behold,
A beginner's grace—if only it was bold!

We imagine a show, with flair and style,
But end up in heaps, laughing all the while.
Dressed in layers, we guffaw and fidget,
Crafting memories, the tale we will credit!

Frozen Lullabies

Beneath a blanket of shiny sheen,
A penguin sings, looking quite keen.
He tries to waltz on frosty ground,
But ends up tumbling all around.

A polar bear joins in the fun,
With silly moves, he weighs a ton.
They slip and slide, what a sight!
All through the frozen, gleaming night.

Echoes of Soft Night

In the dark, where the chill winds blow,
A squirrel dances, putting on a show.
He twirls and spins on icy trails,
While a sleepy owl hoots and exhales.

Beneath the stars, laughter will rise,
As frosty friends pull silly ties.
They trip and flip, what a dream,
In the night, they all laugh and beam.

Silvery Stillness

A rabbit hops in pajamas tight,
Slips on a patch, oh what a sight!
He bounces back, with giggles galore,
Falling flat, he laughs some more.

With glistening ice and stars aglow,
A raccoon joins the muffled show.
He juggles snowballs, oh what a treat,
But they fly back, landing at his feet.

A Dance of Light and Frost

In the moon's glow, a dance begins,
As snowflakes swirl, and winter spins.
The snowman winks and takes a leap,
While giggles echo, oh so deep.

A fox with skates glides along,
Sings a tune, but it’s all wrong.
He twirls around, with laughter bright,
In a chill that warms the frosty night.

Hushed Crystals

In a winter's night, they shimmer and gleam,
Dancing around like a frozen dream.
Snowmen wobble, with carrots askew,
As slippery penguins slide right on through.

Laughter erupts with each playful fall,
As hot cocoa spills, making a mess of it all.
Icicles giggle, their shapes so absurd,
While frostbite whispers, 'You haven’t been stirred!'

Frosty friends stomp, their boots overly large,
In a comedic march, all feeling the charge.
Chasing their hats, which wander away,
In the chilly frolic of a winter’s ballet.

But when the bells chime, announcing the freeze,
They all take a tumble, with grace, if you please.
A skit on the ice, a joyous pirouette,
Ending the night with no signs of regret.

Shatter in Starlight

Beneath twinkling stars, the snowflakes play,
Laughing and spinning, they don't care to stay.
A squirrel in a hat, very proud and quite bold,
Tripped on a shiver, his mischief retold.

Each glide on the ice turns into a show,
Where llamas in skates put on a grand throw.
Juggling snowballs, they tumble and sway,
Cracking up snowflakes along the way.

Frozen fish gossip, with bubbles in tow,
While penguins in bow ties put on a fast show.
Waddle and twirl, they take to the stage,
In this frosty festival uncaged from their cage.

As the night winds down, they grin and collide,
With frosty fizz drinks, in a joyful slide.
Leaving behind a trail of bright glee,
On this hilarious stage that’s made of icy spree.

Glimmers in the Dark

Beneath the stars, a dance begins,
Penguins twirl amidst their spins.
A snowman dons his finest hat,
While frosty squirrels chat and chat.

Icicles hang like toothy grins,
As rabbits wear their cozy pins.
The air is crisp with laughter's tone,
Where frosty antics freely roam.

In chilly gusts, a snowflake prances,
Frogs on ice take daring chances.
As winter chips at frozen ponds,
All gather 'round to dream in fronds.

With every slip and every slide,
The icy ground sings songs of pride.
So raise a toast to joys we find,
In winter’s grip, so sweetly kind.

Icy Reveries

A walrus sports a shiny bow,
While penguins line up in a row.
They slip and slide, a clumsy crew,
Creating joy in chilly dew.

A snowball fight breaks out with cheer,
As frosty friends all gather near.
Their laughter trails like sparkling streams,
In the kingdom of ice, it's all in dreams.

The northern lights do wink tonight,
As frosted critters bask in light.
A lonely polar bear took flight,
But all he found was pure delight.

Charmed by frost, they dance around,
With every fall, another sound.
In winter’s play, the world feels free,
Like frozen fun for you and me.

Frozen Elysium

Amidst the snow, a party's planned,
With flavors cool, a taco stand.
The foxes grin and munch away,
While icy winds play hide and stay.

A penguin juggles lanterns bright,
While rascally owls hoot with spite.
The air is thick with fluffy cheer,
As frosty friends draw close and near.

Glittering flakes on noses rest,
The chilly breeze puts dreams to test.
As snowflakes fall with laughter's glee,
Their joy spills forth, like waves at sea.

Each frosty paw leaves prints of fun,
In Frozen Elysium, spring's long run.
So let us toast with mugs of chill,
To laughter's warmth, it rocks our will.

Chilled Serenity

A marshmallow king on frosty throne,
Waves to a crowd of fur and bone.
The winter air, a canvas clear,
Where laughter dances, full of cheer.

A sledding side-swipe brings delight,
As kids in jackets take to flight.
The snowflakes whirl, a joyful race,
As chilly winds grant every place.

Hot cocoa spills, a comical spill,
With whipped cream splatters, what a thrill!
The icicles swing like disco balls,
As snowmen melt from the laughter calls.

In chilly serenity we bask,
With snowball fights, the fun we'd ask.
So come enjoy the frosty plight,
Where every laugh is sprinkled bright!

Enchanted Stillness

A squirrel slipped on frosty ground,
With a graceful twirl, he quite unwound.
Snowflakes giggled in chilly air,
As penguins danced without a care.

A cat in boots strolled by with glee,
Chasing shadows as they flee.
The stars above peered down to see,
Who would win the winter spree.

A bunny hopped with comic flair,
Ended up stuck in frozen hair.
With flailing legs and wild eyes,
He made the moonlight laugh and rise.

Whispering Fragments

The icebergs cracked with silly sounds,
Echoing jokes from snowy grounds.
A walrus grinned, his tusks all bright,
Telling tales of his snowy flight.

A fish with hat did swim around,
Wearing winter gear, so profound.
He twirled and spun in every direction,
Creating bubbles in a new connection.

A seal on skates did twirl and glide,
While otters cheered from the icy side.
The winter night was never a bore,
With laughter ringing forever more.

Fortunes of the Night

A pair of foxes played a game,
Sliding down a hill, oh what a shame!
They hit a tree, then found their luck,
Riding branches like they were struck.

The moon above watched with delight,
As snowmen danced into the night.
A carrot nose took flight at last,
While snowflakes fell, making it fast.

Chickens roamed in coats of snow,
Clucking tunes in a rhythmic flow.
When they tripped and slipped with squeals,
Their plumpness made the night surreal.

Radiance Beneath the Stars

An owl wore glasses perched so proud,
Reading jokes to a sleepy crowd.
The stars above winked in surprise,
As laughter sparkled in their eyes.

A moose wearing rollerblades,
Zoomed past trees in icy cascades.
He tried to stop, but oops, he flipped,
With a belly laugh, the night was gripped.

Beneath bright skies, friends gathered round,
Sharing snacks on the frosty ground.
As giggles echoed, the night glowed bright,
In whimsical chaos, all felt right.

Celestial Chill

Under the stars, we glide with glee,
Twisting and turning, like fish in the sea.
Frosty days if we're bold and bright,
Skating on clear paths, oh what a sight!

With laughter loud while tumbling down,
We slide and squawk, our faces a frown.
Jackets puffed up like marshmallows round,
Each wobble a dance, new moves to be found.

Our breath in the air, like dragons we puff,
Spinning and tripping, we can't get enough.
The ice calls our names, “Come give it a try!”
Even if you fall, just laugh, don't cry!

Frostbitten toes and noses all red,
But who cares when there's fun to be had?
We'll conquer the chill with a giggle and cheer,
Under the stars, it’s all crystal clear!

Frigid Glow

Dancing around like penguins that skate,
We shuffle and slide, it’s never too late.
Socks in our boots, oh what a delight,
Tiptoe on ice, we glide through the night!

Hot cocoa spills as we race to the edge,
I’ll challenge you first, let’s call it a pledge.
But watch out for me, I’m slippery and sly,
I might just trip you, oh my oh my!

Shiny blue blades, we're flapjacks on ice,
Wobbling like jelly, it’s not very nice.
We fall and we giggle, our cheeks all aglow,
Creating a spectacle, the best winter show.

With frosty fingers and bright shining eyes,
Contests of who has the best silly lies.
As we skate through the evening, I feel joyful and bold,
This frigid glow is more fun than gold!

Lusters of Stillness

I slipped on the surface, the night turned to day,
Like a banana peel, I'm going to sway.
Ice acting like glass, oh so dignified,
But watch out for me, I’m clumsy with pride!

Whispers of wind make the air feel so grand,
We swirl like snowflakes with no master plan.
Our laughter erupts, like bells in the night,
Each tumble a triumph, a comedic flight!

Glowing with laughter, we twirl through the chill,
Sprinkling snowflakes, making our hearts thrill.
As we leap and we play, ever so free,
The luster of stillness is pure jubilee!

And though we may tumble and fall like the leaves,
Our spirit stays high, each giggle achieves.
In the wonder of winter, we find joy and a jest,
Lusters of stillness? We’re having the best!

Winter Illumination

Tip-tap on ice, our dance is a blast,
With moves like a pro, or falling—so fast!
Twinkling like stars, we're dressed up so nice,
Finding new ways to slip on this ice!

Shoe laces are tangled; I can’t find my socks,
But look at that fellas doing strange flocks.
The cold nips my nose, but who really cares?
When friends have your back, it’s the fun that shares!

Frosty air biting, yet spirits won't sink,
We cheer and we howl, over chocolate we clink.
With laughter like echoes, we glide with delight,
Creating a ruckus, oh, what a sight!

Under the glow of the lanterns aglow,
We sparkle and shine, together we flow.
Our joy fills the night; it’s a pure celebration,
In this crazy winter, is there hesitation?

Frozen Dreams Beneath Stars

In a world where penguins wear hats,
They slide around on ice, oh so sprat.
Snowmen dance with chocolate canes,
While polar bears play silly games.

The stars above just giggle and shine,
As snowballs fly through a frigid divine.
Elves on skates sing jingle bell rhymes,
While gingerbread houses bake in good times.

Shimmering Silence

Whispers of snowflakes fall with a spree,
As squirrels in mittens climb up a tree.
A tiny deer dons a scarf for the show,
While frozen fish form a slick, frosty row.

Laughter erupts from a bubbling brook,
As ice skaters slip with a comic hook.
They twirl and they spin, all giggles and grace,
A clumsy ballet in this frosty place.

Celestial Dance on Crystal

In a place where yetis do cha-cha and slide,
Snowflakes twirl like dancers, with vigor and pride.
The owls hold a party, with cookies and cheer,
As snowmen do splits, making all of them leer.

Jelly beans tumble from clouds in the fray,
Yetis shout, 'Catch them!' as they frolic and play.
The ground starts to shake with a ticklish tune,
While penguins breakdance beneath the bright moon.

Luminous Shadows in Winter

A rabbit wears glasses, so eye-popping bright,
He conducts ice skaters, a marvelous sight.
With chocolate syrup and whipped cream galore,
His winter wonderland opens the door.

Giggling shadows dance under the stars,
As snowflakes giggle, ‘Don’t land on the cars!’
A penguin slips, and the crowd bursts in cheer,
While a bear spins around, pulling off a grand steer.

Frost-kissed Dreams

In the frozen field, a penguin pranced,
With little shoes on, he took a chance.
A snowman winked, with a carrot nose,
As chilly winds danced in winter's clothes.

Beneath the stars, a squirrel did slide,
Wearing ice skates that he had tried.
He twirled and slipped, a comical scene,
As frosty giggles echoed serene.

The rabbit hopped, with a jolly cheer,
While chasing snowflakes that disappeared.
With each bounce, he left a trace,
A frosty face in the playful space.

Under the stars, the critters planned,
A wild ball where they would stand.
With laughter bright and spirits high,
They celebrated beneath the sky.

Ethereal Glow

A cat on ice, with a hat too small,
Chasing its tail, it takes a fall.
It rolled and tumbled, a furry sight,
Laughing at itself, what pure delight!

An owl up high, in the evening chill,
Spied on the antics with quite a thrill.
Winking and hooting, it cheered the show,
As creatures danced with a twinkling glow.

A bobcat tried to join the fun,
But slipped on a patch where the frost had run.
With a comical thud, it joined the crowd,
As all the forest laughed aloud.

For in this glow of chilly cheer,
No one's too cool to lose their beer.
With snowball fights and a silly pose,
They savored life, as laughter grows.

Celestial Silver Dance

The stars in the sky had a giggling chat,
While mice on skates did a spin like that.
With tiny bows, they took their stance,
Launching into the celestial dance.

A fox in tights turned out to prance,
Attempting ballet, but lost his chance.
He leaped too high, then crafted a dive,
With a flair like no other, he felt alive.

Down came the snow, a soft confetti,
Making each twist and turn quite ready.
The moon giggled, showing its face,
At the cosmic shenanigans in outer space.

In this wild waltz with a sparkling dose,
The stars clapped hands, as laughter arose.
Each animal spun, each creature charmed,
Creating a joy that left them disarmed.

Frigid Whispers

From the chilly woods came whispers low,
As icy winds began to blow.
A raccoon whispered, 'Let’s play a game!'
'Till frostbite steals our sassy fame.'

A troop of bunnies jumped on the ice,
Trading somersaults for a roll of spice.
They giggled and squealed, their ears all akimbo,
As a bear joined in, in a bouncy limbo.

But then came along a clumsy moose,
Who slipped and fell with a funny bruise.
He dusted off snow, then took a bow,
Saying, 'Winter shivers, but I’m fab now!'

The frost held secrets, the night wore lace,
While laughter echoed all over the place.
In the realm of cold, their spirits soared high,
With frigid tales that would never die.

Frost's Enchantment

Chilly breezes make us squeak,
As we grab our toes that peep.
Slipping, sliding with delight,
In this frosty, twinkling night.

Snowmen dancing, hats askew,
Waltzing with the icy dew.
Hot cocoa splashes, marshmallows fly,
Laughter echoes, oh my, oh my!

Shoveling pathways, what a chore,
Then we stumble, crash – it’s lore.
With each fall, the giggles grow,
Who knew winter could steal the show?

As the sun gets swallowed whole,
Watch the snowflakes, what a goal!
Painting laughter with each breeze,
On frost, we slide like silly seas.

Stars on Frosted Glass

Little lights in the night sky,
But our breath makes the best high.
Drawing faces on the pane,
Suddenly, they dance in vain.

Snowflakes land, a lacy tease,
Tickling our noses, if you please.
We catch them, giggling with glee,
“Look! A snowbird!” Oh, can’t you see?

Footprints leading to the fun,
Sliding down the hill, we’re done!
Sleds flip over, laughter spills,
We’re just kids with wild, big thrills.

In this wonderland so bright,
We’ll forget the chill of night.
With hot chocolate, joys arise,
Frosted windows, laughing eyes.

The Winter's Whisper

Whispers chill beneath the moon,
Yet our cheeks blush like a balloon.
Jackets zipped and hats pulled tight,
Waddling snowmen take to flight.

Racing boys and girls on snow,
Who can balance? Oh no, oh no!
The ground gives way, a sudden fall,
Laughter bounces, that's our call!

Carrot noses that wobble so,
Eyes made of coal, they steal the show.
With snowballs thrown in joyous play,
We dodge and weave, hip hip hooray!

Even the trees wear a winter grin,
As we spin and twirl, feeling kin.
A winter's tale, so full of cheer,
With each giggle, we hold it dear.

Ethereal Frost

Chilly nights and twinkling frost,
Wonders of winter never lost.
With every step, we slip and slide,
Snowflakes twirl like a wild ride.

Bundles of scarves and laughter loud,
Guess who fell? The silliest crowd!
Rolling snowballs, round and fat,
Oops! A snowman’s wearing that hat!

Dancing shadows, a rhythm prance,
Every slip’s just part of the dance.
Hot drinks cover our goofy spills,
But our laughter easily thrills.

With the stars, we cheer and sing,
As jumping through snow is our ring.
Ethereal moments, frosty delight,
Every giggle shines through the night.

Glacial Threads of Light

A dance of sparkles on the pond,
Where laughter echoes, joy's a bond.
Slipping around with a cheeky grin,
One falls down, but then stands to spin.

The chilly breeze whispers a jest,
As snowflakes land on heads, no rest.
Snowball fight turns into a chase,
Who knew winter could hold such grace?

Feet fly wide, but none take flight,
With merry giggles, the world feels right.
Hot cocoa waits for those who fall,
Let's warm our hearts, the best of all.

Celestial Frost

Stars are winking, the sky's in play,
It’s cold, but we’ll survive the fray.
A snowman sports a carrot nose,
Chasing our dreams, where laughter grows.

Icicles hang like a choir's tune,
We sing out loud, under the moon.
Tumbling over, we roll and slide,
Belly laughs echo; it's a wild ride.

Frosty air, with a giggle or two,
A chilly prank, what'll we do?
With frozen fingers and rosy cheeks,
We dance about, what fun it seeks!

The Illuminated Chill

Bright lights twinkle on the frozen ground,
Each step we take, a creaky sound.
Frosty fingers, a friendly poke,
In this chilly land, we laugh and croak.

Sliding boots on a slick terrain,
One will fall — oh, the comedic pain!
Furry hats bob, all are awry,
With joyful hearts, we raise our cry.

Each breath we take a misty plume,
As we frolic midst the winter bloom.
Hot drinks waiting with marshmallows piled,
In this frosty fun, we feel like a child.

Melodies in the Snow

A winter symphony plays outside,
Where jolly spirits tumble, slide.
We toss and giggle, throwing bright snow,
A chorus of laughter in a cheer-filled show.

The chilly dance brings shivers of glee,
Falling down, whoops, let’s blame the tree!
Wrapped in layers, we waddle around,
Singing our praises, such joy we've found.

Snowflakes tickle, the night feels bright,
Under the stars, everything’s just right.
Hot soup is waiting as we stroll,
In this wintry wonder, we find our role.

Starlit Crystals

In the chill of the night sky,
The snowmen start to sigh.
With carrot noses out of place,
They dance in a silly race.

Laughter echoes through the frost,
While penguins claim they've lost.
An ice slide made of lemon zest,
Turns winter's chill into a jest.

Squirrels wearing tiny skates,
Share jokes on frozen plates.
Round the tree they take a spin,
Their acorn hats fly off with a grin.

As icicles start to freeze,
They sprinkle jackets on the breeze.
With giggles freezing into air,
The frosty fun is everywhere!

Shining Whispers of Winter

The flakes like dancers swirl around,
In this icy, whirling sound.
Snowflakes tickle noses bright,
As snowmen honk, that's quite a sight!

A bunny wearing shades of pink,
Thought ice would make him sink.
Instead, he slides and slips with flair,
Squeaking tunes of frosty air.

Icicles laugh while they hang low,
Whispering secrets from below.
The owls hoot comically in tune,
Funny shadows of the moon.

With every pitter-patter beat,
The world feels cold yet sweet.
In winter's grip where fun takes flight,
Joy twinkles in the night!

Gleaming Pathways of Night

On a path of icy smudges,
Even the dogs wear fuzzy pudges.
They slip and slide like fools on parade,
Chasing tails in the frosty glade.

The snowflakes take a tumble and roll,
Creating a wintery hole.
As kids giggle and dogs play tag,
The sleds zoom fast, glad to brag.

Stars above twinkle with glee,
Watching all the fun from a tree.
A penguin brings hot cocoa near,
But spills it with a comic cheer!

The night is bright with frosty laughs,
In this magical place, winter crafts.
With every chuckle that takes flight,
It's a silly, shining delight!

Fragrant Frosted Air

In the air a scent so sweet,
Pantries filled with winter treats!
Gingerbread cookies, fresh and round,
In frosting battles, laughter's found.

Snowflakes land on noses pink,
As snowmen pause and start to think.
What's better: scarves or much more cheese?
The crowd erupts with joyful wheeze!

The frosty world, a candle bright,
With giggles sailing into the night.
Polar bears in matching hats,
Dance like never before, oh look at that!

In fragrant air where fun takes flight,
The cold can't clash with such delight.
With every chuckle, with every cheer,
This merry winter brings us near!

Night’s Crystal Veil

Under the sky, a dance unfolds,
With penguins slipping, oh so bold!
They waddle and twirl, in frosty glee,
While laughing at their clumsy spree.

A parrot squawks from a nearby tree,
"Don’t slip, my friends, it’s quite funny!"
But there they go, a wild cascade,
In this chilly world, their plans are made.

The stars are giggling with every fall,
As frosty friends have a giggle ball.
Their icy antics, pure delight,
In the shimmering chill of the night.

With each glimmer of stars up above,
A frosty party, a dance of love.
In this whimsical winter scene,
Jokes are shared, and hearts are keen.

Shimmering Echoes

A snowman sneezes, the others freeze,
With frosty flakes a-jumping like peas!
They chuckle and giggle, hats askew,
A comedic sight, what can they do?

A well-armed fort made of ice and snow,
Snowballs fly high, like a brace of arrows!
"Hit the snowman!" the children shout,
But he just waves, full of frost and doubt.

The wind whispers tales of slippery fate,
As sleds zoom by at a rapid rate.
A dog in a scarf, he joins the chase,
Dashing through snow with a goofy face!

The moon's laughter echoes in the air,
As boots get stuck in the frozen lair.
While friends fall over, knees of white,
In this shimmering chaos, pure delight.

Silvered Serenity

In a field of glitter, they gather around,
Chasing their shadows, they trip on the ground.
A troupe of oddities, with flair they prance,
Missed every cue in the frosty dance!

A cat in a scarf, shivers and purrs,
As wise owls giggle, puffing their furs.
Every step is a slip, a twist, and a shout,
While the laughter builds with every flout.

The skaters glide, with grace gone awry,
One leaps to spin, but lands on the guy!
With a splash and a dash, as laughter ensues,
They find their joy in the playful blues.

Beneath the starry blanket stretched wide,
Silly stories are shared with pride.
In the quiet glow, with each cheerful cheer,
Silvered serenity brings laughter near.

Dusk's Icy Embrace

Balloons wobble by on a frosty gust,
With giggles and snorts, they are packed with thrust!
As kids start to tumble, their cheeks all aglow,
The moments we cherish, while winter winds blow.

Hot cocoa spills, a dribble on snow,
As marshmallows tumble, putting on a show!
The crowd erupts with laughter and glee,
A splendiferous carnival, wild as can be.

A team of snowflakes dance in the breeze,
While the jolly old man tries hard not to sneeze.
He juggles and slips, with light-hearted grace,
In dusk's icy hold, all mischief takes place.

Glistening echoes of laughter abound,
With rosy-cheeked faces, joy knows no bound.
Under starlit skies, the fun never ends,
In this sparkling realm, where the laughter transcends.

Moon's Icy Caress

A penguin slid with grace and glee,
It wore a hat, oh so fancy!
The frosty floor was its big stage,
While others just watched in a daze.

A snowman danced with a wobbly spin,
Chasing a squirrel, oh how he grinned!
But slipped on ice, became a heap,
And the crowd roared, they'd never sleep!

A polar bear tried to do the jig,
With a twirl so grand—even did a dig!
But hippo's laugh was the loudest cheer,
For costume mishaps are what we hold dear.

So here we twirl, and laugh in delight,
As frosty evenings bring laughter bright!
Through chilly nights, the joy won't cease,
In this chilly wonderland, we find our peace.

Celestial Shimmer

The stars winked at a snowy field,
Where rabbits joined in to dance and yield.
They hopped and twirled with quite the flair,
And left little paw prints everywhere!

With each new leap, they had a ball,
While a squirrel chuckled, watching them stall.
He’d thrown some snow, a cheeky ploy,
As the rabbits squeaked 'Oh what a joy!'

A llama slipped, tried to join the show,
But found its legs in a flurry, oh no!
It rolled and tumbled, a fluffy mess,
And laughter erupted—what a success!

So under the stars, we laugh till dawn,
As bunnies bounce and the fun goes on.
In winter’s glow, our sweet retreat,
A stage of giggles, so pure and sweet.

Echoes in the Frost

The owls hoot out a silly tune,
As the critters gather beneath the moon.
A raccoon dons its snazziest wear,
While two little foxes pull off a dare!

They skated ’round on a chilly pond,
With giggles and jigs—a joyful bond.
When one slipped under, a splash arose,
And snowflakes danced like comedy prose.

A moose attempted a belly flop,
But landed soft—oh how we'd stop!
The frost cracked smiles, a comedy spree,
As laughter echoed in harmony!

So gather ‘round, let the stories flow,
Of tumbled friends in frosty glow.
With whimsy and warmth, we dance tonight,
On the edge of laughter, ‘neath stars so bright.

A Tapestry of Light

In a patch of snow, good friends appear,
With cocoa mugs and lots of cheer.
A snowball fight, the air so crisp,
But cheeky Billy gave them all a lisp!

With one sly toss, it hit the cat,
Whose startled jump was quite the spat.
The laughter rang as he slinked away,
While squirrels plotted for another play.

A dancing snowflake had lost its groove,
And wobbled crazily, trying to move.
With giggles high in the frosty ether,
While everyone shouted, "Just be a bleeder!"

So let's embrace this winter show,
Where every slip brings a warm glow.
In a vivid tapestry, we'll weave our night,
With laughter and warmth, a pure delight!

Frozen Luminescence

The pond was a disco, all shiny and bright,
With skaters in costumes, what a silly sight!
They glided like penguins, then slipped with a cheer,
As laughter and giggles echoed so clear.

A snowman in shades danced by on the ice,
Calling all snowflakes to join him, how nice!
They twirled in the glimmer, missed a step or two,
In a frosty ballet, oh what a view!

Hot cocoa in mugs, they toasted with glee,
To the giggly fairies who joined the spree.
Then one cheeky skater, with flair in his spin,
Landed square on his face—letting fun win!

With snowballs in hand, they charged with delight,
A frosty free-for-all, what an epic night!
The stars joined the fun, they winked from above,
As ice turned to laughter, it fit like a glove.

Hallowed Chill

Under the shimmer of frosted delight,
A raccoon in flippers skated with might.
He slipped on a banana peel, plaid shorts on hand,
Declared it a dance move that none could withstand.

The owls were hooting, providing the tune,
While rabbits all wobbled in line like a swoon.
Juggling hot potatoes near snack time for sure,
Resulted in laughter, and chaos—no cure!

An ice patch disaster? What a glorious fall,
As everyone toppled, they giggled and sprawled.
The frosty concoction of friends in a race,
Created a scene that would melt any face.

So raise up your cups, let good times ignite,
For frosty gatherings bring joy to the night.
The hallowed chill sparkles, with laughter in tow,
As friendships grow warmer in snow's lovely glow.

Shards of Nightfall

Beneath the night's twinkle, a party took flight,
With penguins in bow ties, oh what a sight!
They slid past a snowman with a top hat and flair,
While munching on ice cream, without a care.

A squirrel on skates wobbled on by,
Challenging shadows to give it a try.
He tumbled, he chuckled, and jumped up with cheer,
Saying, "Who knew that the cold could bring beer?"

A troop of young snowflakes began to conspire,
To pull off a prank that would surely inspire.
They piled up the snow in a mountain so high,
Then slid down its side like a fantastic pie!

The shards of night fell in bursts of delight,
As each frosty mischief led to laughter so bright.
Nights like these spark joy under starlit seas,
With friends making memories, and snowflakes to tease.

Sparkling Secrets

In a land made of glitter, the ice began to sing,
As squirrels shared secrets, while doing their thing.
With tackle-boxes filled with fish-flavored snacks,
They skated in circles, giving no one a whack.

A chipmunk stood tall, with a crown made of snow,
Proclaiming, “The ice is where clowns come to glow!”
The crowd chimed in choruses, that tickled the air,
While ice skates transformed to a three-ring affair.

With each little slip, a giggle arose,
As everyone wondered what makes laughter grow?
Is it cold, is it sparkling? Is it falling on ice?
Perhaps it’s just friends, being oh so nice!

So gather your giggles, and share them with glee,
In evenings of magic, where all can be free.
The secrets we keep in the chill of the night,
Are treasures of joy that just seem to ignite!

Celestial Frost Pictures

In a world so white and bright,
The penguins slip, oh what a sight!
They waddle around with grace so wide,
Trying not to take a frosty slide.

With snowflakes dancing, they start to play,
Building castles, hip-hip-hooray!
A snowball fight, who will win?
With laughter echoing, let's begin!

The stars above seem to chuckle too,
As ice skates twirl, with a shoe or two.
One penguin slips, that's how it goes,
Descending down on frosty toes!

So grab a sled and let's dive deep,
In this winter land where we seldom weep.
Under the chilly, giggly sky,
We're all just kids, oh my, oh my!

Secrets Illuminated by Night

When the frost creeps softly near,
Fish tell stories, bright and clear.
A snowy owl hoots, 'Hey, what’s that?'
While squirrels sneak out, wearing a hat.

The stars are gossiping, a stellar chat,
About a bear who danced like that.
With paws so big and feet so round,
He slipped and crashed without a sound!

Nearby, a rabbit’s having a ball,
Jumping high and starting to fall.
Into a bush, all fluffy and spry,
While the nightingale chirps, “Oh my, oh my!”

In this frozen land full of cheer,
Wild tales unfold as critters appear.
Secrets splashing like snowflakes bright,
In the whimsical fun of the night.

Lunar Reflections

On a pond that glitters like stars,
Frogs in tuxedos drive tiny cars.
They croak their tunes, not missing a beat,
While fish throw parties, oh isn't that neat!

A wise old turtle makes a slow dash,
He'll join the dance but first take a snack.
With a boom of laughter, the night takes flight,
Frogs do the cha-cha under the starlight!

The beavers tap their tails in glee,
As they waltz with ducks, two and three.
The reflections swirl, what a sight,
A gala beneath the twinkling light!

When the sun peeks in with a knowing grin,
The party's over, let's do it again!
With bubbles of giggles, off we glide,
In the fun of the night, we'll take stride.

Glistening Shadows

As the shadows stretch and yawn,
The raccoons plan a midnight dawn.
With masks on faces, so sly and cute,
They gather snacks—oh, what a hoot!

The icy ground is slick and clear,
But with some slips, there's nothing to fear.
A snowman's hat flies high in the air,
While one raccoon jumps without a care!

Through the trees with a jolly skip,
They search for treats, one little trip.
With giggles echoing through the night,
Chasing moon shadows, what pure delight!

So raise a toast, to friends so sly,
With frosty mugs that sparkle and fly.
In glistening laughter and snowy cheer,
We laugh our way through the frosty year!

Dance of Frozen Radiance

In a winter wonderland so bright,
Penguins twirl, giving quite a fright.
With flippers flapping, they take a chance,
Slipping and sliding in their merry dance.

Snowflakes giggle as they tumble down,
Each spin adorned with a frosty crown.
A snowman cheers with a carrot nose,
As the penguins flaunt their frozen clothes.

On a patch of ice, they all get bold,
Playing tag while the stories unfold.
“Watch my jump!” one proudly proclaims,
And lands on his buddy, but who’s to blame?

To the rhythm of winter, they prance and glide,
With giggles and laughter, they take it in stride.
In the chilly air, their spirits ignite,
Creating a ruckus in the shimmering night.

Icy Harmony

Beneath the stars, a chilly brigade,
Frolicking freely, not one is afraid.
A polar bear leads with a chubby grin,
While a laughing seal joins in the spin.

They're ice skating on a giant cake,
A slip and a slide, oh what a wake!
“Is that a fish?” one dolphin does shout,
Adding to the fun, as they zoom about.

Whales serenade with a honking tune,
While owls hoot softly, beneath the moon.
With flutes made of icicles, they play,
As critters gather for this frosty ballet.

The frozen stage, a multitude of cheeks,
All rosy and jolly, in thermal peaks.
“Let’s do the conga!” the squirrel declares,
And everyone dances without any cares.

Radiant Solitude

On a lonely peak, under glimmering frost,
A lonely raccoon thinks he's a boss.
With mischief in his heart, he takes a leap,
Only to find the ice is too steep.

He slips and slides, as he tries to look cool,
While singing off-key in a frozen pool.
"Hey, watch this move!" he proudly cries,
And promptly bumps into a pair of surprised eyes.

A fox in a hat, with a smirk so sly,
Chuckles at the raccoon, as he wobbles by.
"Your dance needs a tune," she slyly quips,
As he twirls around, doing backflips.

In this quiet space, with icicle trees,
Friendship blooms, like the softest breeze.
They giggle and chatter, forgetting the chill,
Adventures unfolding, with laughter to spill.

Gleam of the Night

Under a sky where starlight glows,
A moose trips over his own two toes.
“Look at me!” he shouts, a bit out of sync,
As he tumbles headfirst into a cold drink.

The beavers chuckle, building a dam,
While the owl hoots, “You’re quite the jam!”
They laugh at the moose, in his sparkling mess,
Calling him “Beverage King,” no less!

The night is alive with such jolly refrains,
As friends gather round, ignoring the pains.
With hot cocoa flowing from a leaky jug,
They toast to the fun with a big, warm hug.

In the cool of the night, camaraderie grows,
With sparkles and giggles, victory glows.
So let’s join the party, both furry and bright,
As we dance through the flavors of joyous delight.

Celestial Frost

Under the stars, we slip and slide,
Our laughter rings, like a joyride.
Snowflakes dance, bold and bright,
Wearing our mittens, what a sight!

Hot cocoa spills, oh what a mess,
Falling down in winter's dress.
Bunny slippers fly through the air,
Chasing friends without a care!

Frosty noses and silly pranks,
Jumping waves in icy banks.
A snowman's hat, it rolls away,
While we burst into a playful sway!

But as we chill, let this be clear,
We'll laugh until the next warm beer!
Frosty toes and frozen cheers,
Sipping smoothies still brings jeers!

Chilling Radiance

A sparkle here, a slip there too,
We glide around, what can we do?
Banana peels on icy paths,
Giggles burst like winter laughs!

Glowing orbs in the chilly night,
Tickling toes, oh what a fright!
With every tumble, we just grin,
These frosty games, how to begin?

Wobbly legs and swirling spins,
Our frozen dance makes no one win.
Chilly cheeks, a rosy hue,
At this ice party, come join the crew!

Yet here's a twist, like cream's surprise,
Hot pies await beneath the skies!
With each cool moment, a cozy bite,
We're laughing hard till morning light!

Gleaming Winter's Calm

Stars above in a chilly sea,
We sing and skate, wild and free.
Snowflakes wink, they say hello,
As we roll around, moving slow!

With chattering teeth, we throw some snow,
The tallest snowman begins to grow.
What’s that? A carrot that just fled?
Chasing it down while we laugh, we tread!

Slipping here, oh my, oh dear,
Our ice capades bring forth a cheer.
Those frozen feet do dance away,
“Hey! Be careful!” we laugh and play!

Although we slip, we’ll slide with grace,
Flopping happily, we find our place.
With chills and fun, we end our night,
Each frosty grin a pure delight!

Reflected Solitude

On this slick floor, we find our groove,
Chasing shadows as we move.
With ice skates sharp and giggles wide,
It’s a wild journey, come take a ride!

The moon above glows, but here below,
We turn and twist, putting on a show.
Hot fish sticks dance on icy flares,
Craving warmth in our snowy lairs!

A tumble here, a giggle there,
Laughter echoes, fills the air.
Frosty breath makes shapes that soar,
Join the fun, there's so much more!

Though we slip like frozen fools,
We make our way through winter's rules.
So grab a friend and let’s collide,
The frosty fun, our snowy ride!

Silver Gleam on Frost

In the cold, the ground does wink,
Slick and shiny, grab a drink.
Skating fast, I take a dive,
My nose is red, but I feel alive!

Friends all gather, laughter loud,
One slips down, we cheer him proud.
Sprinkled in snow, a confetti show,
Who's the graceful one? No one knows!

Chasing shadows in this frost,
We laugh so hard, the giggles lost.
Remembering when shoes would fly,
Rooted firmly, unable to try!

With silver gleam, we dance around,
Belly flops and faces on the ground.
Who knew that slipping could be such fun?
Oh, let it snow, let’s do it again!

Whispering Reflections

Under stars where laughter roams,
I glide past and steal the homes.
Mirror images, one and two,
Who's the best? Definitely not you!

Everyone thinks they're a skating star,
But then I trip, and it's quite bizarre.
Spinning round like a topsy toy,
End with a laugh, oh boy, oh joy!

Shadows sway as we take a twirl,
Falling gracefully like a pearl.
Funny scenes in a frosty play,
Wipe those tears — it's a laugh today!

Whispering tales of our grand falls,
Tip-toeing near ice castle walls.
Chasing echoes of our delight,
Splashing joyfully into night!

Enchanted Chill of Night

Beneath a sky of sparkly dreams,
We skate and giggle, no it seems.
Frosty air, but hearts are warm,
Watch your step, or be the charm!

Who needs a rink when you have a street?
Slippery bets on our frozen feet.
I scream with glee as I take a fall,
Laughter surrounds, we have it all!

Clad in jackets, all fluffy and bright,
We prance and step, what a funny sight!
I twist and fumble, what a bold move,
With a flip and a spin, it's the comedy groove!

Under enchantment, laughter rings,
Joking about our skateboarding flings.
Hold my cocoa — and watch me go,
Whoops! there I am, laying in the snow!

Ethereal Glow Above

Glows from above, the night's allure,
Underneath we fumble for sure.
Echoes of joy fill the chill,
As we chase thrills, it's quite the spill!

Cocoa spills, and we laugh anew,
Pass the marshmallows and we chew.
Skating lines twist, then tangle a lot,
Oh, look at you! You just got caught!

Shimmer and shine, the stars do tease,
Sipping hot drinks, we catch a breeze.
Jumping and spinning, we dare the frost,
Yet every tumble is laughter embossed!

Ethereal moments, dressed up in glee,
Chasing our dreams, so wild and free.
Under the sky, we dance with delight,
Every slip brings a new funny sight!

Seraphic Winter's Touch

In winter's grasp, we glide with glee,
Snow pants on, and hot cocoa spree.
With each silly slip, we laugh and squeal,
As frosty flakes challenge our balance to heal.

The penguins mock with their daring grace,
While we tumble down, a comical race.
Snow angels formed with our flailing limbs,
A laughter chorus, where no one hims.

With snowballs thrown like marshmallow fluff,
Sledding so fast, it's never enough.
Caught in the drifts like a rookie mountaineer,
We raise our mugs high and toast winter cheer!

So bring on the chill, the shiver, the fun,
With sparkling light, winter's joy has begun.
Let's dance in the snow, wear smiles so wide,
For in this frosty wonderland, we'll abide!

Sapphire Skies

Beneath the blue, we twirl and spin,
Shining like diamonds, let the games begin.
With laughter bubbling like fizzy delight,
We'll prance in the snow 'neath the stars so bright.

Our frostbitten toes tap a choral song,
As we waddle like ducks, all silly along.
Spirits lifted, we chase fluffy flurries,
With cheeks like tomatoes, there's no need for worries.

The snowmen giggle with their carrot-grin,
While we create snowballs to pelt with a spin.
"Take this!" I shout, as I hurl through the air,
Only to trip, rocket-falling without a care.

Yet here in the cheer, our hearts find their place,
In this magical world, we find endless grace.
With sapphire skies above and laughter around,
It's a winter wonderland where joy knows no bounds!

Glimmering Frostbite

On frosty nights with shivers galore,
Ice skating stumbles, oh, what a chore!
We flail like fish, slipping with glee,
While giggles erupt, just wild as can be.

The frosted air bites, but oh, what a treat,
With hot cider warming each frozen little feat.
We trip and we tumble, a slapstick ballet,
As frozen gnomes lay in our frosty ballet.

Sleds go zooming with an acrobatic flair,
Who knew snow could launch us into the air?
We land with a thud, covered head to toe,
In a glittering blanket, creating a show.

With winter's cold breath tickling our skin,
Laughter resounds, it’s a riotous win.
So gather your friends, let's embrace this delight,
In a world of frost, we’ll dance through the night!

Chilled Reflections

With frozen ponds holding secrets so bold,
We trip on the ice, but oh, we’re not cold!
We throw in some snowflakes, a sprinkle of fun,
As we slip, slide, and twirl, joy has begun.

Our cheeks are rosy, our laughter is loud,
Skating in circles, feeling so proud.
But who needs control when we can be free?
Flopping and flailing is the key, can't you see?

Some skate with grace like a swan in a lake,
While we create chaos, for goodness’ sake.
Gentlemen with style, they slip on their toes,
And here we are, in our shimmery clothes.

So lift up your mugs, toast to winter’s delight,
Where laughter and hiccups brighten the night.
In this chilled escapade, we find our resolve,
Dancing on ice, with joy’s sweet dissolve!

Whispered Luminescence

The night is bright, the ice is slick,
I slipped and spun, what a neat trick!
My dog just laughed, he thought it grand,
As I danced around, with no helping hand.

A penguin strolled, with quite the flair,
Waddled right past me, without a care.
I tried to follow, I lost my grip,
Spinning and twirling, oh what a trip!

The stars above twinkled in glee,
Watching my antics, oh how they see!
With every fall, I let out a squeal,
As laughter echoed, it felt so surreal.

So here I am, in this frosty bowl,
Trying to keep my pride, but oh, I stole
The limelight tonight with my clumsy fate,
Dancing on ice, oh, isn’t it great?

Frosted Nebula

Amidst the frost, the air was still,
I took a step, I took a spill!
My friends all gathered, pointing and yelping,
While I lay sprawled, my dignity melting.

The stars above shared a knowing glance,
As I struggled hard to regain my stance.
A snowball flew, I ducked too late,
And my cosmic clumsiness sealed my fate!

A yeti appeared by the frozen stream,
Challenging me to a frosty dream.
But as I leaped, I slipped on a bear,
Twirling around like I didn't care!

With giggles and joy, the night rolled on,
We laughed so hard, until the dawn.
For in this chill, some warmth I found,
In every fall, love spun around.

Shimmering Nightscape

The sky glowed soft with a playful gleam,
While I attempted to live my dream.
But one little slip, and oh what a mess,
I landed square in my wooly dress!

A twinkle of stars above shook in mirth,
As I spun around, feeling light as a firth.
My glee turned to giggles; my patience wore thin,
Yet the laughs from my pals made my spirits win!

A snowman chuckled with a carrot nose,
As I danced with joy in the icy prose.
With every slip, I turned it to play,
Gliding through night in a hilarious way.

So here's to the falls and the scrapes we share,
As the chilly air fills with comedic flair.
For in this shimmer, warmth will ignite,
Making memories bright on this sparkling night!

Glinting Serenity

Under the stars, I take a glide,
With a cheeky grin, I'm slipping with pride.
A friendly snowball flies through the air,
And lands with a thud—well, isn’t that fair?

A snowflake dances; I try to catch,
But instead I’m wearing ice like a patch!
The moon chuckles low, it’s all in good fun,
As I dress in frost, I think, “Well, I won!”

The dog took off, he’s racing the breeze,
With fur aflight, he dodges the freeze.
We chase each other, all laughter and skill,
As the glimmering ice bends to our will.

So here I remain, with my frosty attire,
Sharing a moment that warms like a fire.
In the glinting night, we forget all our woes,
In this snowy dance, our laughter just grows!

Frostlight Fantasia

Beneath the sparkle, shoes take flight,
A penguin dance in the pale moonlight.
Snowflakes giggle, falling with glee,
As snowmen chuckle beneath a pine tree.

In icicle hats, the squirrels parade,
Sliding on ice like they're just made.
Tiptoeing over the slippery floor,
One snowman crashes, oh, what a roar!

Frosty noodles hang from the eaves,
Giggles echo, chattering leaves.
The scene is set for a frosty tease,
With snowball fights that aim to please!

Toasty marshmallows by the fire,
With icy jokes that never tire.
Each frost-covered prank brings joy anew,
In this land where chilly dreams come true.

Shining Frosts

A frosty flashlight made of snow,
We catch the light and let it go.
Fingers slip on the frozen ground,
As everyone giggles at strange sounds.

Snowman dressed in a winter cape,
Tripping over his carrot shape.
The chill brings laughter, spread out wide,
As we stumble like penguins in the glide.

Tracks of a cat leave a comical trace,
Sliding and spinning, oh what a race!
With icy hugs that leave us in stitches,
We tumble and roll like star-studded witches.

But wait, what’s that, a pizza afloat?
A dream made real in a frosted coat!
We’ll feast on the snow and dessert galore,
In this winter fun, there’s always more!

Crystalline Nightfalls

Under a glimmer of frosty cheer,
A bear on skis gives a silly leer.
With twinkling eyes that shine so bright,
He slides past trees that giggle in fright.

A snowflake tickles a laughing pup,
Chasing his tail, oh, what a sup!
Catch me if you can, the frost seems to say,
As icy giggles lead the way.

Frosty friends in a frozen square,
Building a castle with whimsical flair.
A snowball fight breaks out with delight,
And laughter rings through the crisp night.

Up on the hill, a sled takes flight,
With two tiny mice that giggle with might.
They soar through the air with a joyful twist,
In this winter realm, how could we resist?

Secrets of the Winter Sky

Underneath twinkling stars, we play,
A glistening slip in a snowball ballet.
Elves in shorts on a ferocious sleigh,
Zoom past the snowmen, hip-hip-hooray!

Chasing the ice with a cola in hand,
We laugh as we slip, oh isn't it grand?
The chill of the air, yet warmth in our hearts,
As we partake in these frosty arts.

Polar bears giggle in oversized gear,
Making snow angels, spreading the cheer.
Every tumble and fall is a cause for a prank,
Beneath the frosty night, we took the plank.

Secrets abound in the frozen night,
With frosty confetti that sparkles so bright.
Hot cocoa smiles in the chilly game,
As we chase down the winter, never the same.

Frost-kissed Serenade

Underneath the frozen gleam,
A penguin slips, oh what a dream!
On ice he twirls like a ballet star,
Wishing he drove a slick little car.

Snowflakes fall, they tickle my nose,
A snowman laughs, in his frozen clothes!
He waves a stick, his carrot askew,
As I slide by, yelling, "Watch out, dude!"

A polar bear in a scarf so bright,
Waddles by with all its might.
He dances, he prances, a fuzzy delight,
While I cling to my skates, trying not to fright!

Chasing each other beneath the stars,
Laughing and joking, forgetting our scars.
What a sight, with the ice all aglow,
Who knew fun could be so slippery, though!

Twilight’s Glimmering Veil

A squirrel skates down the silver freeze,
With little acorns, he’s aiming to tease.
His little legs go wobbly and wild,
Like an overexcited and very small child.

Frogs in tuxedos croak out a tune,
They bring the party under the moon.
With top hats that look just slightly askew,
They hop and they flop, giving a boo-hoo!

I glide past a snowman with shades so cool,
Who’s sipping hot cocoa, acting the fool.
“Can I join?” I ask, as he offers a cup,
“Just don’t belly flop; it’s hard to get up!”

The owls are hooting, invoking a cheer,
While igloos shake with laughter and beer.
What a sight under the bright moon's ray,
Ice is slippery, but fun's here to stay!

Icy Radiance

The moon shines down on a frozen lake,
While seals are plotting some mischief to make.
With a wink and a nudge, they start a slide,
Trying to dodge a very grumpy tide.

A squirrel in skates goes zipping by fast,
On an icy ramp, will he manage to last?
He flips and he flops, then lands with a thud,
Rolling on ice like a fluffy little bud.

The fish are all laughing behind glassy walls,
As comets of snowflakes take graceful falls.
A crab in a tutu takes center stage,
Has everyone seen the new dance craze?

While snowmen chuckle with saucy delight,
They spin around for the glamorous night.
Fun is the name of this frosty affair,
I'll bring the hot cocoa, if you bring the flair!

Night’s Glacial Embrace

In the chill of the night, a skater does twirl,
While a cactus in gloves gives a whirl and a swirl.
“Is it cold?” he asks, as he shivers with glee,
While ice creams melt with a plea to be free!

A walrus gets tangled in sparkling lights,
And slips on the ice with all of his might.
Flopping around with ridiculous grace,
“Just call me Elvis!” he shouts, what a face!

Snowflakes powder the jogging fruit bats,
As igloos throw parties in wild winter hats.
The owls are gossiping, oh what a show,
Tales of the penguin who put on a glow!

So here’s to the madness wrapped in cold cheer,
With laughter and fun, let’s all sing it clear!
Winter’s a canvas for silly, a bliss,
So join the parade—who could ever resist?

The Quiet Chill

The night is cool, but me? I'm warm,
Wrapped in blankets, feeling like a charm.
Sipping cocoa, my tongue's a mess,
I dream of sliding—oh, what duress!

Outside there's laughter, kids zooming by,
I trip on my own feet, oh my, oh my!
A slip, a slide, who needs to stand?
The snowman chuckles, I just can't land!

With each little tumble, I start to grin,
This frozen ballet? I'm sure to win!
I cartwheel in snow, like a frozen seal,
Just pass me a snack, that's the real deal!

The stars above twinkle, they see the play,
While I'm here acting, in a silly display.
Grab your hats, folks, come join the fun,
For tonight's our stage; let's make this run!

Starry Fragments

Under glittering skies, the air is bright,
In this chilly wonder, we dance with delight.
I clutch my hot drink as I try to prance,
Who knew that cold could feel like a dance?

A snowball flies by—“Hey, that’s not nice!”
I return the favor, oh, think twice!
Each throw’s a giggle, each fall's a cheer,
Nature's a circus, and we’re the deer!

Frosty noses meet a crunching sound,
With every misstep, we lose all ground.
My friends start to wobble, then stumble too,
And suddenly, there’s a snowman crew!

Starlight grins down on our frosty parade,
We’re rebels of winter, and we’re unafraid.
Let's make snow angels, with flair and jest,
In this icy kingdom, we’ll never rest!

Glacial Serenade

In the still of night, as the snowflakes creep,
I see a penguin, do I dare to leap?
A slip of the foot? That's part of my charm,
Just dance with me, nothing here can harm!

With marshmallow hats and noses so red,
We skitter and scatter, no tears to shed.
Sleds zoom past, like jellybeans on ice,
Hold onto your cocoa, not once but thrice!

The frost creates music—can you hear the tune?
A symphony of giggles beneath the moon.
A chorus of friends, all bundled so tight,
With wobbly moments, we're a true delight!

The snow sings softly, as we swirl around,
Wrapped in the laughter, so carefree, unbound.
So here's to the night, with sun still in sight,
A frozen fiesta, everything feels right!

Twinkling Frost

Glimmers of frost, like confetti they fall,
I trip on my skates, and it's all my fault!
With a spin and a topple, I land on my back,
The snow’s my soft pillow; oh, what a knack!

Friends gather ‘round with popcorn in hand,
Casting snowballs, can’t make a stand.
A new winter sport, we’ll call it a game,
The laughter and cheer will forever remain!

With a clatter and crash, we challenge the night,
Who can make snowmen? Oh, what a sight!
Busted noses and giggles, unplanned accents,
In this frosty wonder, we build our defense!

Stars wink down at our snowy delight,
Daring us onward, as we giggle and fight.
So grab on your friends and let’s make a toast,
To this frozen playground, we cherish the most!

Milton Keynes UK
Ingram Content Group UK Ltd.
UKHW022007131124
451149UK00013B/1049